A pocket book on
HOUSEPLANTS

David Longman

First published 1982 by
Octopus Books Limited
59 Grosvenor Street
London W1

ISBN 0 7064 1608 2

Produced by Mandarin Publishers Ltd
22a Westlands Road, Quarry Bay, Hong Kong

Illustrations: Pru Theobalds

CONTENTS

Plants in the home

In the world at large plantlife plays a vital role in maintaining the ecological balance. On a smaller scale, plants can transform homes, offices and shops by adding freshness, colour and movement. They provide a relatively inexpensive and potentially spectacular form of decoration which offers an infinite variety of combinations. Plants may be used in mixed bowls, in groups, or as single specimens for maximum dramatic effect. Use them to give atmosphere, to create illusions of depth and breadth and to camouflage unattractive features.

Most plants are not very demanding and, once you have taken the trouble to learn how to take care of their basic needs, they will repay you handsomely for your efforts.

About the book

In this book we have tried not only to give some ideas on the use of plants in the home, but also helpful hints on containers, tools, feeds, displays and buying plants. Another section deals with pests and problems that trouble most houseplant growers.

The second half of the book contains an A-Z guide to most of the popular houseplants that are currently on the market. This gives the common and botanical name, useful information about room conditions, ease or difficulty of culture, light, temperature, propagation of young plants and which pests and diseases are most common to a particular plant. Together with a drawing to help identify the plant, this section should enable a would-be purchaser to decide which species will be suitable for their own home, and within their capabilities.

A little advice

Growing plants indoors is not difficult; it can be great fun and give a great deal of satisfaction. Do no start with either too many or too difficult plants, for it is so easy to get depressed and despondent if plants die prematurely.

Start with one or two plants in the easy category. When these have been mastered gradually acquire some of the medium or difficult ones.

Furniture and plants

Most people collect plants in a haphazard way, buying what they think they can grow rather than thinking about the plant's impact on the room in which it is to be placed.

A plant should be part of the decor of the room in which it is to live, and to this end it must blend into the overall effect.

After a little practice in looking after plants, you can start buying them for specific purposes — for example, to enhance the appearance of a certain room or part of the house. Fair-sized plants do this most dramatically — say, a large palm in a sitting room, a dracaena cane on a landing, a hanging plant basket of philodendron scandens in a bathroom.

Match plants to furnishings

Modern furniture requires distinct, angular leaf and stem shapes; perhaps just one or two large plants standing in matching containers, chosen to tone in with the room.

Victoriana requires fussy plants in small bowls and pots, placed on tables, bureaux or sideboards. The containers should be varied, and often ornate. Mixed displays in unused fireplaces look charming in this sort of setting.

Country or cottage type houses needs plants tumbling from windowsills or ledges. Again, mixed bowls and wicker containers suit this decor.

Never put a plant where it is going to obstruct movement; plants don't like being jostled any more than people do.

Light

Remember, all plants require light and some need more than others. If the most attractive setting for a plant is in a place away from all natural light, consider fitting an artificial light to be left on most of the time. Special horticultural bulbs that aid plant growth are available.

Camouflage

Plants can be used to hide an ugly feature, like protruding pipes, bad brickwork or simply an empty, uninteresting corner. Always experiment with different plants to see which one fits best into any situation.

Indoor gardens

Beside a floor-to-ceiling window, a plant bed can be built, so that it appears to flow out of the house into the garden, with the window as a divider. If carefully planted, the bed can give the effect of bringing the whole garden into the house. On a smaller scale, window boxes, placed inside the house and carefully positioned to receive the maximum amount of light, give a fresh look.

Indoor beds

When building an indoor bed, make sure that it is water-proof. Thick polythene, available for lining garden pools, will normally be sufficient. For safety, use a double thickness. Alternatively, the brick interior of the bed can be plastered and covered with waterproofing bitumen paint. Removable galvanized metal containers can be made to fit the bed.

The bottom should contain 5 cm (2 in) of drainage material, such as gravel or broken pots, and be sprinkled with charcoal. Fill the bed with a mixture of half potting compost and half peat. Allow the bed to settle for about a day before planting.

Plants and windows

As already mentioned, indoor gardens should be built as near a window as possible. This allows plants to receive the maximum light available. If tall plants are being grown, they will throw attractive shadows and light patterns into the room and can provide the shade necessary for some smaller plants that dislike strong sun light.

Mirrors

To enlarge an indoor plant room, consider facing one wall with mirrors. This gives an illusion of great depth, particularly with the reflection of leaf patterns. Spotlights focussed on selected plants highlight a display and at the same time help growth. Take care that no leaf or stem actually touches the light or is too near the light source; it may be burnt.

1. Codiaeum
2. Citrus mitis
3. Capsicum
4. Aphelandra
5. Hedera variegata
6. Hibiscus

Cactus and succulent gardens

All cacti are succulents, but not all succulents are cacti. Cacti can be distinguished from other succulents by the small tuft of felt or hair at the base of the spines called an areole. The spines are partly for protection and partly to help the plant gather moisture from dew in the desert — its natural home.

General care

Cacti and succulents can both survive a lot of neglect, but will flourish and flower regularly if given attention. They should be treated as normal houseplants in summer and watered frequently. They require plenty of air, and in the winter time should be allowed to dry off. They flower after new growth and prefer to be pot-bound. Plants over three or four years old should produce flowers every year.

How to plant

Cactus gardens are always popular and are best planted in a shallow bowl to allow little root growth. Use a potting compost mixed with an equal quantity of sharp sand and choose plants to give a mixture of shapes, sizes and textures. A suitable selection would be opuntia, espostoa, echinocactus, cereus and rhipsalis.

The top of the dish or bowl can either be dressed to look like a desert with sand, gravel and one or two small protruding rocks; or in the style of a Japanese garden, with little ornaments such as figures, bridges, temples and a mirror. To complete these gardens, top dress with coloured stones.

Looking after the garden
Cactus gardens should be watered sparingly, as there is no natural drainage in a bowl and cacti will rot if water-logged.

Dust by using a small, soft brush, but be careful as the spines of the cacti can be dangerous.

Showing off your plants
When looking for containers in which to show off your plants, remember that all plants, with the exception of cacti, enjoy a certain degree of humidity. In the house you can provide humidity by putting several plants together in a container so that they will give each other moisture, creating what is known as a micro-climate. This can be done in conventional plastic or glass fibre troughs and containers. These modern containers fit well in some decors — but often there is scope for using something more unusual.

The first requirement is that the containers are water-proof or can be made so. Secondly, the plants must be arranged so that the container is not completely hidden, or alternatively just hidden enough to make the casual visitor look a little closer to see what is holding the plants.

Unusual containers
military kettle drum (with military crest)
Victorian hip bath
wooden or wicker cradle or small cot
coal or log buckets
children's or miniature wheelbarrows
old Victorian or Edwardian cooking pots or pans
old foot bath
lavatory pan
lavatory cistern

Terrariums
Terrariums date back nearly 150 years to an accidental discovery by a scientist. Whilst studying the development of a moth chrysalis, he also discovered that plants would germinate and grow in closed glass cases. His experiments showed that a whole variety of tropical plants flourished and the terrarium was soon put to practical use for transporting newly discovered plants by ship from the tropics to Europe.

Today terrariums are becoming popular again. They often resemble miniature Crystal Palaces, and normally have a hinged or removable panel for easy planting and maintenance. Unfortunately, because they take time to construct, they are expensive to buy, and the beginner would be well advised to consider other glass containers first. Small fish tanks or round fish bowls are excellent, as are old, well washed acid battery containers. In fact, anything with glass sides and either no top or a removable one would be ideal.

Planting the terrarium

No special equipment is required, but an essential point to remember about a terrarium is that you must be able to get at least one hand into it.

To plant, place about 1-2.5 cm ($\frac{1}{2}$-1 in) of gravel on the bottom and mix in about 55-85 gr (2-3 oz) of charcoal. Cover this with blotting paper or newspaper. Next, add at least 5 cm (2 in) of potting compost with 25 per cent extra peat added. Press down firmly and water. Leave for a day, then plant with small plants, arranged to suit the container.

Always choose small and relatively slow growing plants. Be careful not to over-water, as this can cause rotting, because the water cannot evaporate.

Suitable plants	
fittonia	peperomia
pilea	dracaena red edge
saintpaulia	adiantum
cryptanthus	pteris
	chlorophytum

Bottle gardens
The culture of plants in terrariums and bottle gardens is very similar. The principle of cultivation is that the high sides of the container restrict evaporation and moisture runs back to the compost to maintain humidity.

Bottles to use
The old glass chemical containers, known as carboys, were first put to use. The tall, round shape often magnified the plants for a startling effect. Unfortunately access to the plants through the narrow neck is difficult. Other suitable containers are sweet jars, glass brandy balloons, candy jars or large, clear wine bottles. It is also possible to buy jars made especially for bottle gardens.

Tools
To cope with the difficulties of planting, weeding and pruning in bottles, many people improvise tools. Household forks, razor blades and spoons can be wired on to thin bamboo canes to provide home-made equipment.

Planting
Planting, compost and plants are exactly the same as for the terrariums. If the opening is narrow, use a funnel

made of paper or card to insert the compost. It should only be necessary to water once a month. If a plant appears to be growing too fast, be ruthless and remove it.

Hanging displays

Hanging baskets are always an attractive way of displaying plants and are particularly useful when space is limited. However, they can be difficult to maintain and become a nuisance inside the house if they drip water. The conventional basket is made of wire (sometimes plastic covered) and lined with moss. When assembling, line the basket with green florists' moss and then put in a piece of polythene. Add potting compost, water well and plant.

Indoor baskets
For indoor use, there are plastic baskets with a drip tray attached underneath. When planted carefully, the basket and tray will be hidden by trailing plants.

Outdoor baskets
Plant with summer bedding plants, such as trailing geraniums, and hang outside the house. Water daily, otherwise it will dry out and the plants will die. Remember, this type of basket drips when watered.

Suitable plants for indoor baskets

chlorophytum	rhoicissus rhomboidea
philodendron scandens	scindapsus
hedera helix	columnea microphylla
tradescantia	

Suitable plants for outdoor baskets

petunia	impatiens
trailing lobelia	variegated ivy
ivy geranium	calceolaria
fuschia	zebrina
nasturtium	sedum
begonia	

Macramé hangers
Macramé-style hanging cord containers made of string, jute, wool, beds and many different materials make very attractive holders. Some of these hangers will take two or three plants in vertical display. Plant a mixture of hanging plants and some of the more upright plants, especially in hangers designed to take more than one basket. Always put a drip tray inside the hanger to catch drips. Take care not to damage the leaves of plants when inserting or removing them.

Climbing and trailing plants as room dividers

Modern living rooms are often multi-purpose areas. Frequently one part has to be screened from another, for example a dining area to be separated from the sitting area. Plants are an excellent way of decorating a shelving unit used as a room divider or for simply forming a screen of greenery. If using plants as room dividers, make sure that you leave enough space around them to ensure that they are not knocked or damaged as people move around the room.

Furniture units

Many modern multi-purpose furniture units with shelves and cupboards lend themselves well to plant display. Often small plant boxes can be fitted as an integral part of the unit. If high up, these could contain trailing plants, such as hedera, trailing philodendron, chlorophytum or rhoicissus. Set the boxes at different levels to get a broken pattern of plant shapes.

Troughs

Troughs standing on the floor or on short legs make good room dividers, if the plants in them are tall, or trained up supports. A framework of clean bamboo poles, tied together in a square or diamond pattern with natural raffia, makes a good support. Start with biggish plants to get an immediate cover. Remove plant growth carefully from existing poles or sticks, then tie on to the new framework. Allow plants two or three days to adjust themselves to their new position. If the trough is positioned in a middle of the room well away from the windows, make sure the plants can receive enough light.

Suitable plants for room dividers

climbing	trailing
rhoicissus rhomboidea	tradescantia
hedera	philodendron scandens
fatshedera	chlorophytum
syngonium	scindapsus aureus

bushy	specimen
dracaena	monstera deliciosa
philodendron bipinnatifidum	ficus benjamina
codiaeum	ficus robusta
nephrolepsis exaltata	kentia forsteriana

Bulbs

Bulbs, especially spring ones, are only passing visitors to the house, so why not plant some up in small pots. A single hyacinth or two or three daffodils can then be placed in existing bowls or troughs of green plants to bring a little extra colour on a dull winter's day.

Forcing bulbs

Forcing bulbs to flower is an art that can be easily learned. There are only a few basic rules to follow.

Always buy top quality bulbs. Inferior bulbs will not flower or will produce a weak bloom. If the varieties recommended in this book are not available, consult your local gardening centre.

Most bulbs require a period in the dark after planting in compost, in the late autumn or early winter. Either plunge the bowls in the garden under peat or ashes or leave in a cool, dark cupboard for about two months. Take out the bowl and cover it with a sheet of newspaper. Remove the paper when the bulbs begin to sprout and replace it with a cone of newspaper for about a week; then remove that. Keep the bulbs moist at all times but don't over-water. Tip surplus water out of the bowl. Never try to force the flower by heating on a radiator nor to force bulbs twice — it doesn't work. Plant them out in the garden after flowering.

Hyacinths

Hyacinth bulbs are one of the favourites for forcing. By careful planting (and date labelling) you can have flowers from Christmas until spring. For early flowering, buy what nurserymen call prepared bulbs. If planted in August, they will flower in December. For bulbs you want to flower from January onwards ask for good 'top size' bulbs.

Hyacinths can be mixed, but to make sure that they flower together plant bulbs of the same colour in one pot. Hyacinths also do well when grown in water. Fill a hyacinth vase to about 1 cm ($\frac{1}{2}$ in) below the bulb and watch the bulb sending out its roots to look for moisture. A hyacinth vase is illustrated on page 18.

Daffodils and narcissi

Daffodils and narcissi also force well, but do not flower as early as hyacinths. Plant two layers in a pot, as shown above, to make a really concentrated display of blooms. Suitable varieties are Carlton, Golden Harvest and Fortune daffodils. For narcissi, try Geranium, Cragford and Scarlet Elegance.

Tulips

Tulips must be left much longer in the dark. Don't start to force them before mid-January. The scented doubles like Peach Blossom and Orange Nassau, force well.

Both tulips and daffodils need to be staked when in bloom to stop them drooping.

Small bulbs

Some of the small bulbs can be easily forced, such as iris reticulata, all the crocuses, scillas and chionodoxa. Plant them close together and move them out into the garden immediately after the flowers have faded.

Natural flowering

There are also a number of bulbs that will flower naturally in the house or conservatory. These are all members of the lily family — amaryllis, valotta, nerine and lilium. They all need to be planted permanently in pots and not disturbed too often. They also require a rest period after flowering when they should be allowed to dry off completely.

Buying plants

Houseplants have become so very much a part of our everyday life that they are now available from all sorts of retail outlets, florists' shops, garden centres, specialist plant shops, supermarkets and even motorway service stations. It is difficult to say which is the best place to buy your plants. Much depends on what type of plant you wish to purchase and for what reason. One general piece of advice is to make sure the shop cares properly for the plants it is selling and maintains its stocks in a healthy condition.

Where to buy
Supermarkets and motorway shops often have a limited range of inexpensive plants. They depend on a fast turn-over to keep their stocks in good condition. Garden centres, florists and specialist plant shops are certainly better for the more unusual plants and especially for larger and more showy specimens. It is here that you would expect to find not only a wider range of varieties but also a considerably greater choice of individual specimens.

Market stalls
Be very careful about buying plants from a stall in a market, especially in winter. The effects of a touch of cold may not be apparent until your new purchase is at home in the warm. Although not all stall-holders are unreliable, some are able to offer apparent bargains because they clear wholesale markets of the leftovers, or crop remnants, some of which may be unfortunately far from perfect.

How to choose
It is important to have an idea of where you are going to put your plant before you buy it. Otherwise you may choose a lovely specimen for which you can find no suitable place. If you plant is for a windowsill, then you don't want a fern. If it is for a dark corner, then a colourful flowering plant won't do. Think about a plant's heat, light and air requirements carefully.

Avoid difficult plants

If you are a beginner in collecting plants, don't be tempted into the realms of gardenias, stephanotis or other exotics. There is nothing worse than watching a plant die before your eyes and not knowing why. Unfortunately, the more exotic a plant looks, the more difficult it is to look after. Many variegated and brightly coloured plants, such as caladium, codiaeum, begonia rex and maranta, may take a little getting used to. It is best to stick to all green plants to start off with. If you have success with these, you can then try your hand with their variegated relations. If the label on your plant says F_1 hybrid, this means it has been grown from two dissimilar parents. It will be vigorous and showy, but you will not have any success trying to propagate it by seed, because it will not breed true.

Another point worth mentioning is that it is better to avoid oddities, like Venus fly traps, which are generally sold dormant. They will rarely grow into the splendid plants shown on the packaging.

Asking for help

One other piece of advice about buying plants: don't be afraid to ask for help from the assistants. This is where the specialist shops should be able to help you more than the supermarkets or market stalls. A lot of growers now label plants not only with their botanical and common names but also with simple and useful hints about how to care for your plant. If you are worried about the way your plant is or isn't growing, don't be afraid to go back to the shop or nursery; not to complain, but to ask for advice. Do so before the trouble has gone too far, so that there is time to correct the fault, if there is one.

Examining the plant

Once you have decided on the variety you want to buy, it is time to examine individual specimens. The pot should be clean and unbroken, and the compost on top should be fresh and not covered with moss or sprouting weeds. The plant itself should be growing firmly in the centre of the pot and, where necessary, should be securely staked. The stem should be straight and unmarked, leaves clean, smooth, shiny, untorn and healthy. If it appears that some of the leaf tips have been cut off, ask why. Some varieties (like some palms) cannot help making brown tips, and these may have been removed for cosmetic reasons. Lastly, as already mentioned, the plant should be named and preferably have growing instructions.

All this may seem as if finding a sound plant to buy is very hard work. With a little practice you will soon be able to tell good plants from bad. Pick up your specimen, examine it carefully, and think if it will look right in the place you have in mind. Avoid dusty, dirty specimens with a missing leaf that have obviously been on the shelves a week or so too long.

Taking your plant home

The next important thing is to get your purchase home safely, especially if you are buying it in the winter time. Insist that it is correctly wrapped up, if necessary with a double layer of paper. If it is cold, the top of the paper should be fastened over securely. If the plant looks tender or the stems appear too weak, ask for an extra cane to support it so that it is not damaged in transit. Special care should be taken in moving large plants, as a broken leaf or growing tip can spoil an expensive purchase.

Moving house

Another time to give a lot of consideration to your plants is when you are moving house. Often they are put into the back of the removal van with no particular attention at all. All plants, especially large specimens, become acclimatized to one position or room and react badly to being moved. A little care and forethought can keep treasured plants in good health and help them to adapt quickly to their new environment. If possible, place all your plants together in one room a day or so before you move. Believe it or not, they benefit from being close to each other. Then pack them carefully by tying up loose leaves, stems and branches and wrapping the plants in paper or polythene. Pack them in easily transportable cardboard boxes or tea chests, and see that they are loaded into the removal van away from the cold. Unpack them as soon as possible after arrival, and put them together in a warm room before moving them to their permanent positions.

Equipment and materials

It can easily be argued that all you need to look after plants is a milk bottle for watering and a clean piece of cotton rag for cleaning. These are the bare essentials, but, if you a real enthusiast, you will want to know about all the available ways of keeping your plants in good condition. It is not necessary to go out and buy a lot of expensive equipment before purchasing your first plant. The best way is gradually to assemble the various articles, as you need them for your expanding plant collection. You buy only what you really need.

Basic needs

The first piece of equipment to acquire is a good watering can, preferably two, a small and a large one. These should both be the same shape; squat with a long spout that will take a rose attachment. It doesn't matter what materials the cans are made of, plastic and metal are equally good. Next you will need a plastic bucket, which is useful as a portable rubbish bin for dead leaves and faded flowers, for mixing composts or wetting peat. You can fill it also with water to plunge plants like hydrangeas or azaleas.

A good mister is also very valuable to the indoor gardener. If you can, buy two: the first for plain water and/or foliar

feeds, and the second for pesticides. Always remember to wash the mister out thoroughly after using any chemicals, paying special attention to the nozzle. This can easily get blocked by dried chemical salts. If you do have two misters, remember to label clearly which one you are keeping for pesticides.

Adding to the collection

As your houseplant collection grows, so will your enthusiasm, and with it your need for more basic equipment. Other things to add to your store at this stage are a sharp knife, a pair of garden scissors, secateurs, a set of small hand tools (particularly for window box gardeners) and gardening gloves. For tying up indoor plants you will need twine, string, raffia and plant rings. It is also a good idea to keep a reel of wire, bamboo canes and moss poles in stock. If the moss on your poles becomes tired or broken, go to your local florist, buy a bagful and re-moss the pole by tying it on with twine. Lastly, a selection of plastic saucers in all sizes and a variety of pot holders are always useful.

The refinements

If you have a greenhouse or conservatory then a thermometer is essential. The maximum/minimum type is particularly useful in winter, when a sudden drop in

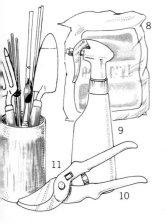

1. Watering can 2. Selection of pots 3. Seed trays 4. Broken crocks 5. Compost 6. Plastic saucers 7. Charcoal 8. Sand 9. Mister 10. Secateurs 11. Tools, cane and brush 12. Plant ties 13. Knife 14. Scissors 15. Raffia 16. Moss poles 17. Plant rings 18. Fertilizer 19. Leaf shine 20. Rooting powder 21. Insecticide

temperature could be lethal to plants. A water meter, to indicate the amount of water in the compost, and a hygrometer, to give you the degree of humidity in the atmosphere, will be your next requirements. To clean your plants you may want leaf-shine. Follow the manufacturer's instructions. There are plants which react badly to leaf shine. Do not use it more than once every two months.

Another important range of equipment is self-watering pots and containers. The basic design comprises a water reservoir with a porous membrane across the top on which the soil and plants sit. The moisture is drawn up by osmosis, often aided by cotton wicks. It is essential to follow the maker's instructions exactly when using these devices.

The last piece of equipment for a keen collector is a propagator. These will be discussed in a later chapter.

Pots

Whenever keen gardeners gather together, the discussion is bound to turn to plastic versus clay flower pots.

The pros and cons of plastic and clay pots

Plastic	Clay
1. Plastic pots come in a wide range of shapes and colours.	1. Clay pots are more limited in colour, but are pleasing for those who prefer a natural look.
2. Plastic pots stand up to rough treatment. If they do break, they can be replaced cheaply.	2. Clay pots break fairly easily and are expensive to replace.
3. Plants in plastic pots need to be watered less often.	3. Plants in clay pots need to be watered more often.
4. Plants in a plastic pot are less likely to become waterlogged.	4. Plants in clay pots easily become waterlogged.
5. Plastic pots are light. Plants may be top-heavy.	5. Clay pots are heavy and do not topple over easily.
6. Plastic pots are easy to clean.	6. Stains may be difficult to remove.
7. Plastic pots are more suitable for modern peat-based composts.	

Compost

The compost you use for repotting plants is important. You can't just go out and dig up a bucket full of garden soil for repotting. It will probably contain weeds, perhaps some pests and be much too heavy for use in a pot.

Loam-based compost
In the 1930s researchers at the John Innes Institute in Britain developed a loam-based compost that would, with some variations, suit most plants. It has become the basis of modern soil composts. This is its composition.

Compost base
7 parts sterilized loam   3 parts granulated peat
3 parts grit/coarse washed sand

Fertilizer
2 parts hoof and horn   1 part potassium sulphate
2 parts super phosphate

The loam should be sterilized, good quality turf, preferably well-rotted. It should also be slightly greasy.

	Compost base	Fertilizer	Powdered chalk
J.I. no 1 is made by adding	0.05 tonne (1 cwt)	113 gr (4 oz)	21 gr ($\frac{3}{4}$ oz)
J.I. no 2 is made by adding	0.05 tonne (1 cwt)	227 gr (8 oz)	43 gr ($1\frac{1}{2}$ oz)
J.I. no 3 is made by adding	0.05 tonne (1 cwt)	340 gr (12 oz)	64 gr ($2\frac{1}{4}$ oz)

Peat-based compost
This was developed in the 1950s. It is normally composed entirely of peat or 10 parts of peat to 1 part coarse sand. The fertilizer additions are very similar to the J.I. base. The principal advantage of peat-based compost is that it is sterile and holds water longer than loam-based compost without becoming stale or stagnant. Being of a more open texture, it allows the roots to grow more quickly. But note that; its fertilizers are soon exhausted and it cannot support large plants. Also, do not firm down peat-based compost.

Watering

The most essential thing to discover about any newly acquired plant is its water requirement. With a few exceptions it is better to let a plant nearly dry out before watering. Develop a regular pattern of inspection, twice a week or even daily if the room is warm. If in doubt, do not water.

When to water

How do you know when the plant needs water? The best way is probably a combination of looking and touching. Often it is possible to tell just by looking to see if the top of the compost is dry, but to make sure, touch the compost and push your finger down into it. If it feels heavy, do not water. After a time you will get to know the particular requirements of each of your plants.

Plants in clay pots normally require more water than those in plastic. If you knock clay pots, they ring like a bell if dry, and give just a dull thud if wet.

Watering is best done in the early morning or late afternoon. Try to avoid midday if possible, because if it is sunny, water splashed on the leaves can cause scorching. Use water at room temperature if possible and avoid using cold water straight from the tap. Most plants prefer rain water, but of course, this is not always available.

How to water

Generally there are two basic methods of watering — from above or by plunging. The first is simply using a can with a longish spout and pouring water on top of the plant. This method can be used with the majority of plants. Be careful with plants like cyclamen and gloxinia and other plants with a central crown. If you wet this, the plant may rot. The plunging method is better for this type of plant. Immerse the plant in a bucket of water up to about 1 cm ($\frac{1}{2}$ in) below the top of the rim of the pot and hold it there for about a minute before removing. Allow the surplus water to drain off before replacing the plant in its normal position. Some plants, like azaleas, hydrangeas and conifers, benefit from having the pot totally immersed. These should be left until air bubbles cease to rise from the compost. Again allow to drain and firm the compost gently down into the pot, before replacing.

Watering Bromeliads
Bromeliads are different in that nearly all varieties (except cryptanthus) like to have the cup or reservoir in the centre of the flower filled with water. This should be changed every three to four weeks.

Humidity
Overhead spraying to increase humidity is another essential to keep plants healthy in the dry atmosphere of a house. Use a mister with a fine spray, so that large droplets do not fall on to the leaves or on the surrounding furniture. If possible, it should be done daily both in summer and winter, except on plants that are resting. Another way of increasing humidity is to place the plant on a saucer of water lined with small stones making sure the water does not touch the bottom of the pot. Alternatively, place the pot into a larger pot and pack the space between with wet peat or moss.

Hydroculture

Hydroculture is the latest and the most scientific way of growing house plants. Quite simply it means growing plants in water. Horticulturists have been experimenting with this method of cultivation for some years. The main problem was to find an inert substance that would support a plant's root system without crushing it and at the same time allow it to grow and expand. Secondly a fertilizer, that could be left in the container permanently without overfeeding or starving the plant, had to be developed. In recent years both these problems have been overcome.

Suitable plants for hydroculture

philodendron
scindapsus
yucca
syngonium
ficus (small-leaved)
chlorophytum
sansevieria

How plants are grown

Plants are grown in a substance called hydroleca, which consists of fire expanded clay particles, and are normally sold complete in ceramic or plastic containers with a water level indicator. The feeding problem has been solved by developing a fertilizer in the form of granules which are placed in the container. Chemical additives in tap water react with the granules and release food to the plant as and when it wants it. The plant cannot be overfed or indeed over-watered. One phial of feed would last a small to medium-sized plant six months.

Problems

Not every plant will adapt to this method of growing. Short-lived flowering plants especially dislike it, but the range of suitable green plants is vast. Be extremely careful in winter, as water drops in temperature more quickly than soil, and roots can soon be damaged, especially if plants are in unheated offices over frosty weekends. Another drawback concerns the rearrangement of your plants. As plants grown by this method should not be taken out of their pots, mixed plant bowls are uncommon. This is, however, compensated for by the fact that large individual plants can be grown in small containers, as a large amount of room for roots is not required.

Watering on holiday

Going on holiday is always a problem, and it is not necessarily best to let a helpful neighbour look after your prize collection while you are away. A fortnight of well intentioned but over-enthusiastic watering could be fatal.

Don't leave your plants shut up in a room. If the inside doors are open they will benefit from a flow of air. Leave them out of direct sunlight and standing next to each other so that they produce their own damp microclimate. An empty bath is a good place for this.

Self-watering devices

There are several kinds. Capillary mats are suitable for plants in plastic pots, but not clay pots, as these absorb too much moisture. There are hollow ceramic ornaments with porous spikes which release water gradually into the compost. You can make a self-watering device with a plastic bottle by piercing a hole through the stopper, upending the bottle and pushing it into the soil. You can also use lengths of thick wool with one end in a jar of water and the other lying on top of the compost.

Feeding

After watering the next most important requirement is feeding. Although all potting composts, other than seed composts, contain fertilizers in varying strengths, sooner or later these are exhausted. To keep a plant growing uniformly it is necessary to feed it.

As with watering it is very easy to overdo it and give the plant too much food, so it helps to learn the requirements of the individual varieties. The first general rule is to feed a plant only when it is actively growing and healthy. Never feed a dormant or really sick plant. If in doubt wait for a short while; it is generally better to underfeed slightly than to overfeed.

Why plants need food

Plants take most of their nutrition from the surrounding soil through the root system, although some can be absorbed through the leaves.

All plants, whether growing in the garden or in the house, need an adequate amount of nitrogen, phosphates and potassium. Nitrogen gives the rich green colour to the foliage, and potassium encourages the production of flowers and general vigorous growth. Phosphates are necessary for a good root system and stem growth.

In addition most soils and composts contain trace elements, minute quantities of calcium, copper, iron manganese, sulphur, zinc and aluminium, which help growth. Houseplants cannot send out roots to fresh soil for their food, so they need fertilizer.

Fertilizers

There are two main groups of fertilizers: organic and inorganic. The organic types can be rotted garden compost, manure, dried blood, bone meal or fish meal. Organic fertilizers are usually activated by bacteria and work more slowly than inorganic ones. Inorganic fertilizers sold under brand names are mostly synthetic or mined and normally come already mixed in various strengths. They are cleaner to use and therefore better suited to the indoor gardener.

Different forms of fertilizer

Fertilizers are available in a variety of forms from liquid to tablet form. Here are some of the different types and the way in which they should be used.

Liquid feed

The most popular kind and, indeed the best selling, is liquid feed. The advantages are immediately obvious. It is clean, easily administered and economical. The instructions on the bottle usually tell you how many drops of feed to add to a given quantity of water. There are several brands on the market, but the most widely known is not necessarily the best for every plant, as the proportions of the ingredients vary slightly.

Foliar feeds

Another kind of liquid feed which is currently popular is foliar feed. It is sprayed on with a mister and the feed is absorbed through the plant's leaves. For maximum effect it should be applied regularly during the growing season and used in addition to regular root and compost feeding. Do not rely on foliar feeds as the main source of nutrition.

Dry feed

There are also dry fertilizers, some of which are spread by hand on the top of the pot. These are particularly advantageous for large plants or mixed beds where a slow rate of absorption is required. Some of the other dry fertilizers are dissolved in water and administered like the liquid feeds. These dry feeds are very good, but more care must be taken to dilute them correctly according to the manufacturer's instructions.

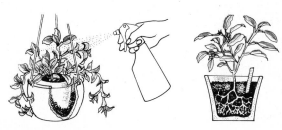

DIFFERENT TYPES OF FEED

Tablets

Lastly, but by no means least, a recent revival is the fertilizer tablet or stick that is pushed into the top of the soil or compost in the pot. This tablet or stick works on the principle that the fertilizer is slowly discharged by the addition of water. The plant gets a regular supply of food over a long period as you water.

Points to remember when feeding

All plants have a resting period when they quite naturally stop growing. Later there is also a dormant period with no growth, when the leaves fall off or the top growth dies down. Usually, though not always, this occurs in winter and plants should not be fed. It is during the growing season, generally from March to October, that plants should be fed to encourage new growth.

When using fertilizers, always make sure to follow the makers' instructions. If anything, be on the mean side. Overfeeding can easily damage the roots.

Remember never to feed a plant after repotting. The new compost should contain enough fertilizer to last about six to eight weeks. Even then no fertilizer should be given if the plant is dormant.

It is a good idea to change your brand from time to time. The slightly differing proportions of the ingredients in another fertilizer may compensate for anything that might be lacking in the one you have been using.

Signs to look out for if:

Overfeeding	*Underfeeding*
leaves split or appear to be scorched	slow growth
summer growth stunted	pale or spotted leaves
winter growth lanky and spineless	flowers small or nonexistent
white crust on top of the soil and on the side of clay pots	weak stems
	leaves dropping off prematurely

Repotting

One of the most frequent questions asked when buying a plant is about repotting. In most cases plants do not need repotting. Reputable nurserymen would not think of selling a pot-bound plant, because if the plant were put into a bigger pot and kept for a couple of weeks, it could grow better and fetch a better price.

Compost

When your plant does eventually need repotting, you will not find it difficult. It is easy to pick up a few simple tricks from the trade. The first essential is to identify in which type of compost the plant to be repotted has been grown. It is important to use the same type of compost. Never repot too soon; if in doubt, leave it for a few more weeks.

Removing plants from pots

The easiest way to tell when a plant is ready to be moved is by its roots. Remove the plant from its pot, by up-ending the plant, placing one hand across the top of the soil and at the same time gently gripping the stem or leaves. Then tap the top rim of the pot against the edge of a table or bench, holding the pot in the other hand. The pot should slide off the plant. Sometimes it is necessary to tap in several places.

At all times handle the plant gently, supporting the stem and foliage with your hands, and remembering you are dealing with a living object. Never bang the pot hard to remove the plant, as you may damage the root system.

Pot-bound plants

The plant that needs repotting has a mass of roots all closely bound together with no soil showing underneath at all: this is called pot-bound. If any soil is showing, do not repot. Other signs can sometimes be seen in the growth. If the leaves go very small and the plant is slow in growing, it may need repotting, although this problem can more often be solved by feeding. Remember, especially with flowering plants, you get a better show of flowers if the plant is pot-bound, especially if it is well fed. The plant puts all its energies into producing flowers instead of new roots. Don't repot just because a plant looks top-heavy or unsightly in a small pot. The problem can often be overcome by placing the whole pot into a bigger one and packing the intervening space with wet peat or moss. This will help with humidity around the plant, as well as improving its appearance.

How to repot

The first step in repotting is to make sure that the plant is well watered. This binds the compost together and helps the plant to withstand the shock to its root system.

Remove the pot as previously described in the inspection. Put the old pot aside to be washed and stored for future use. Now examine the root carefully, looking for any damaged roots or any dead root material. This should all be removed with sharp scissors or secateurs. Gently break apart the roots at the bottom of the ball and carefully remove any crocks or other material used for drainage, again cutting away damaged roots. Now look at the top of the root ball and remove all the compost around it.

Choosing the new pot and planting

The new pot should not be more than two sizes bigger than the old one. Make sure it is clean and dry. Put a layer of crocks or other drainage material on the bottom and cover this with a piece of newspaper to stop the compost blocking the drainage material. Add some compost and lower the plant on to it in the centre of the pot. Supporting the plant with one hand, add a stake if necessary and put in fresh compost up to 1-2 cm ($\frac{1}{2}$-$\frac{3}{4}$ in) from the top.

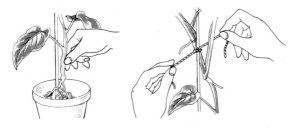

Large plants

These require different treatment if they are too unwieldy to uproot. If you damage the roots you can harm the whole plant, and it is better to rely on feeding than changing the soil. A good alternative is top dressing. With a trowel remove as much of the old soil as possible without disturbing the roots. Look for pests and worms, which should be removed. As with repotting, it is best to perform this operation when the plant is growing. Put in new

dressing to replace the old and firm down. To allow the roots time to get used to the new medium, do not water or feed immediately after repotting or top dressing.

Propagation

Propagation or simple plant reproduction is much easier than most people imagine. Of course there are exceptions, such as bougainvilleas or kentia palms, that require the knowledge and equipment of the expert, but a large number of plants can easily be reproduced without specialized knowledge and equipment. All that is needed is patience and a little care.

It is vastly satisfying to grow a plant from a small seed or tiny cutting. Some plants are propagated merely to increase a collection or to be given away, but others may have to be propagated to keep the strain going. Plants like poinsettias and aphelandras, soon deteriorate if allowed to grow too old, and the vitality of the stock is only maintained by the production of new plants from cuttings or seeds.

Forms of reproduction

There are two basic forms of reproduction in the plant world. The first is vegetative, which involves taking cuttings from stem, leaf or root; dividing of the plant, roots or tubers, and air layering. The other way is by sowing seeds or spores. The majority of house plants are propagated vegetatively, the use of stem and tip cuttings being most favoured, especially commercially. This is also one of the easiest of all methods of propagation.

To get a good young plant it is essential for it to make roots as quickly as possible so that these can provide it with the nourishment it needs to make top growth of stem and leaf.

Ideal conditions

Most indoor plants will root quickly in a high temperature and with a high humidity. Commercially this is often done by placing the propagating beds over hot water pipes and having spray pipes that send out a fine spray of water at regular intervals. This equipment is expensive and difficult for an amateur to install and it is doubtful if it would be worthwhile in most cases. It is possible to make small propagators that are effective and very inexpensive.

Simple propagators

The simplest propagator of all is made by placing the pot containing the seeds or cuttings in a plastic bag and tying up the top. Care should be taken that the bag does not weigh down on the cuttings. You can prevent this by placing a hoop of pliable wire in the pot to hold the bag up. Make another simple propagator by upending a glass jar over a pot; or putting the pot containing the cuttings or seeds into a larger pot, then placing a sheet of glass across the top.

Box propagators

A wooden box with sides about 150 cm (6 in) high and a sheet of glass over the top makes a good propagating box. Alternatively, if more light is required, use four sheets of glass of a similar height held together by wide transparent tape with another sheet across the top.

If you want to use inexpensive materials that may be already to hand, try putting a large transparent plastic bag over a cat litter tray and supporting it in the middle with a milk bottle. With the additional help of a misting spray all these devices produce the humidity required.

Heating devices

Heat is also required underneath to warm the compost. It is possible to buy heating tapes or wires that can be placed in the bottom of your home-made propagator. These should, if possible, be thermostatically controlled and run off a transformer to make them safe. But, it is possible to improvise less expensively. A thick candle burning beneath a metal sheet under the propagator box can be effective. Placing the propagator box on top of the domestic boiler is another method. In a greenhouse, placing the box above a paraffin heater is a good idea. Alternatively, there are on the market a number of propagators complete with heating tapes. Choose carefully particularly with regard to size, because it is easy to buy one that is too large.

Taking cuttings

Taking cuttings is the easiest way of reproducing most plants, and this is usually done with stem and tip cuttings. Take a strong growth (never use weak and straggly growth) and cut off 75-150 cm (3-6 in) with a sharp knife or secateurs. Remove all leaves and buds from the bottom half, dust the cut with hormone rooting powder and place in the rooting compost. Use special seed or rooting compost which is normally fine and contains only a little fertilizer. It is as well to add about a third of sharp sand to improve the drainage. The cuttings should be well watered and then placed into the propagator. Ventilate every day and spray overhead. Rooting time varies from variety to variety but it is often almost four weeks. When the root system of the young plants is apparent, pot up into small individual pots. Many plants can be rooted in water, which makes it easy to see when the roots form.

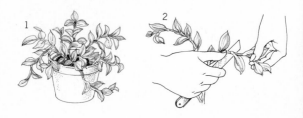

Leaf and root cuttings

Plants like sansevierias and dieffenbachia can be rooted by cutting the leaf or stem into about 10 cm (4 in) pieces and potting into small pots, then placing in the propagating frame.

Begonias and other large soft-leaved plants can be propagated by placing a leaf flat down on the compost and cutting the main vein in several places. Young plantlets will soon form at every incision.

The last method is taking cuttings from roots, especially effective with cordyline. Cut thick pieces of root about 2.5 cm (1 in) long and plant horizontally in seed compost, leaving part of the root uncovered. Keep the propagator at about 24-27°C (75-80°F).

With all cuttings look out for damping off or rotting.

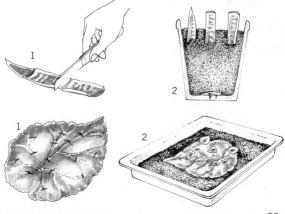

Air-layering

Another more complicated way of taking a cutting is by air-layering. You can use it to deal with a plant that has grown too tall or has lost all its lower leaves. The large-leaved ficus varieties and most dracaenas are suitable candidates for this type of propagation.

How to air-layer

Choose a clean part of the stem and make a shallow incision about 3-5 cm (1½-2 in) long. Dust the wound with charcoal or a fungicide and insert a small pebble or stick to keep the cut open. Wrap some wet moss around the wound and secure with string. Then cover the moss with polythene, tying it as tightly as possible without damaging the main stem above and below the moss. It is a good idea to support the plant with one or two stakes to help it cope with the extra weight and the weakness caused by the cut.

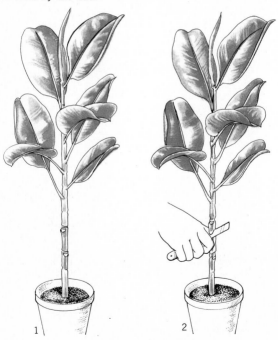

The new plant

After four to six months roots will be seen coming out of the moss on the side of the polythene. Cut the main stem directly below the polythene, dust the wound on the mother plant with charcoal or fungicide and cover the cut with cottonwool or sellotape to stop any bleeding. Then carefully remove the polythene from the top part. If any of the moss is not full of roots, remove that as well. Now gently pot up the rooted portion, taking great care not to damage the young roots. Water the plant and place in a shady place for three or four days. It can help to put the whole pot and plant into a polythene bag to maintain a high humidity.

The old plant

The top of the mother plant's soil should now be changed. The plant will soon throw out young shoots directly below the top of its stump and grow bushy.

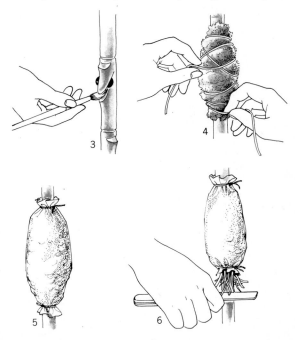

Seed sowing

A different method of propagation is by using seeds. To germinate many house plants high temperatures, controlled humidity and sometimes laboratory equipment is needed. However, there are many plants, particularly flowering ones, that can successfully be grown from a seed. Impatiens, geraniums, primulas, begonias, and grevillea are but a few.

Preparing the container

First choose a clean seed tray and line it with crocks or gravel at the bottom to provide good drainage.

Fill it with fine compost to within 2 cm ($\frac{3}{4}$ in) from the top. Use compost specially mixed for seeds, which contains next to no fertilizer; it helps to add about 20 per cent sterile vermiculite to aid root growth. Firm the compost gently down with the fingers so that it all is of an even

thickness. Then water with a fine spray until it is well soaked. Further watering should not be necessary until after the seeds have germinated. Sow the seeds, either by scattering them, if they are very fine, or by placing them in neat rows, if they are larger. Cover lightly with more compost. Label with variety and sowing date.

Place a sheet of glass over the top and a sheet of newspaper to protect young seedlings from strong light when the first shoots appear. Put the tray in a warm place and wait. Turn the glass over daily to prevent damping off. When the young plants have secondary leaves, pot up carefully into individual pots.

Seeds and pips
There are lots of other plants that can be grown from seeds and pips and kept for a certain time in the house. Most of them are temperate plants, however, and must be put out into the garden sooner or later.

The acorn is one such example. It will soon sprout and within a few weeks a young oak tree will appear. The same is true of fir cones. Place them on top of a bed of peat compost and spray them with water from time to time. Soon the seed will fall out of the cones and germinate and you will have a small forest of young fir trees.

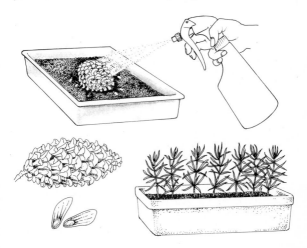

Fruit pips
You can try all sorts of pips; oranges, lemons and grape-fruit are obvious choices. Plant the pips in a pot 2 cm ($\frac{3}{4}$ in) down, water well and cover the top with plastic. About half of the pips should germinate, but remember that they come from large trees and at some stage citrus trees will need a home in a large greenhouse. Date stones can be germinated on damp blotting paper.

Avocados

Avocado pear stones germinate easily even if they do tend to take a long time. It is a good idea to germinate these over water. Push three match sticks into the stone and balance it over a glass of water, with the water just touching the base of the stone. Germination can take up to three months. As soon as the stone splits, roots will grow down into the water and a shoot will appear. Pot up carefully, leaving the top of the stone clear of the compost in the pot. When the shoot has made four leaves, pinch out the growing point. It will then send out side shoots and make a compact bush. The plants can grow quite tall but rarely produce fruit.

Vegetables

Carrots, turnips and beetroot tops can be planted indoors and will soon sprout a mass of green foliage on the top, but in the house this growth is short-lived. It will soon turn yellow and look nasty.

Experimenting with plants like these is popular with children as growth is quick and spectacular.

Self-propagation

Some plants produce young plantlets in the same pot, but separate from the mother, like clivia and caladium. Others reproduce themselves quite naturally during the course of their growth, like chlorophytum. The flowers at the end of the long stem develop into plantlets which can be potted up separately. With bromeliads, young side shoots appear when the mother plant is flowering. These should not be removed until the adult has dried up and died. Ivy, philodendron and ficus pumila all throw out roots which can be pegged down into compost and will soon establish themselves. The new plant can then be severed from its parent.

Division

Dividing up plants is another method of propagation, often used with ferns. Knock the plant out of the pot and break it up carefully into as many pieces as required. Some plants can be pulled apart without too much damage; others need to be cut with a sharp knife before potting. Any cut surfaces should be dusted with a fungicide.

45

Pests and diseases

It is always sad when a favourite plant suddenly looks sick and stops growing. This can happen even to the most expert of growers, but, if caught in time, the problem need not be too serious. Often, particularly with the beginner, it is a result of incorrect treatment.

Normally the appearance of a disease is a sign of poor growth conditions and treatment — like too much water, not enough light, too stuffy a room or too draughty a position. Quick action is necessary. First cut out the affected part of the plant and spray with fungicide. Then consider why and how the plant caught the disease.

Damage can also be caused by pests. These are sometimes on the plant when it is bought, or are transmitted from plant to plant. They may come in on the air and be encouraged by a hot, dry atmosphere.

Golden rules to remember
Common garden pests, such as slugs, snails and caterpillars, can invade the house and eat plants. Remove them by hand and discard mutilated leaves.
Against such pests as worms and small bugs in the soil, use a well diluted mild disinfectant.
Never use infected plants for propagation.
Burn or destroy all infected material. Never place in a compost bin.

Some common diseases
Crown and stem rot The centre of the plant turns soft and rotten and the plant collapses. This fungus spreads quickly and is usually fatal. Throw the plant away. If you catch the plant early, remove the affected part and withhold water temporarily. Move the plant to an airy spot and increase warmth.

Damping off Young cuttings and seedlings collapse at the base through rotting. Remove plants to an airy, cooler position and water with cheshunt compound. Unsterilized compost can often cause damping off, so check the compost before planting.

Grey mould (Botrytis) A prevalent disease, particularly with soft-leaved plants. It is a grey fluffy mould that covers leaves, stems and buds. Usually caused by too much humidity, bad ventilation and too cool a temperature. Remove all affected parts and move to an airy position. Spray with fungicide.

Leaf spot Moist brown spots appear on the foliage of larger-leaved plants like dracaenas, cordylines, dieffenbachia and some philodendrons. It can be caused by bacteria or fungi. Sometimes the spots may become larger, to cover and kill the leaf. Remove the infected leaves and burn. Spray the plant with fungicide. Keep the plant dry and do not mist it for a week or two.

47

Mildew   A white powdery coating which appears under similar conditions to botrytis. Cut away affected parts and soft leaves and wipe off hard leaves. Spray with fungicide or dust with sulphur. Move to an airy place.

Rust   Rust spots form on the leaves. This disease commonly affects pelargoniums. Remove affected leaves and spray with fungicide.

Sooty mould   This often appears in conjunction with aphids, mealy bug and scale. It does not really harm the plant, but it is very unsightly. It can also reduce growth by blocking the leaf spores. Wipe off with a swab dipped in a weak solution of mild antiseptic and water.

Virus   This can affect many indoor plants. The leaves become blotchy and mottled with yellow and growth is stunted. It can be brought on by insects in the soil or can be in the plant when bought. There is no known cure and the plant must be destroyed.

Some common pests

Aphids (greenfly) This is an extremely common, small sap-sucking insect. It is normally green but can also be grey, black or orange. It prefers plants with soft tissue material and goes for young shoots and flower buds. Found in clusters on the stem and underside of leaves. If left untreated, the plant becomes weak and a sticky deposit is found. To treat, spray regularly every 14 days with an insecticide based on malathion or derris.

Mealy bug One of the commonest of pests among hardwooded plants, they are easily controlled if caught early, but difficult to get rid off if they have been allowed to establish themselves. These small insects cover themselves with a cottonwool-like web and nestle in leaf nodes and joints. Spraying with malathion will clear minor attacks, but the best method is to paint out each bug with methylated spirits applied with a small brush.

Red spider mite Another very common pest, particularly with the thicker-leaved plants like ficus, these insects breed very quickly in a hot, dry atmosphere. Regular misting helps to keep this nasty pest at bay. The mites are so tiny as to be invisible to the naked eye, and can be found underneath the leaves where they suck out the sap. The leaves develop yellow blotches and eventually drop off. Webs are also found between the stem and leaves. To treat, spray every seven to ten days with malathion, or derris.

Scale These are small, round, brown insects which look like discs and attach themselves to the underside of leaves, often on the veins. They are immobile and have an outer shell-like casing. They can be gently knocked off a leaf or wiped with a swab dipped in methylated spirits. After cleaning, spray the plant with a malathion insecticide. Sometimes, if a leaf is badly infected, it is best to remove and burn it. If left, this pest will kill the plant.

Thrips These are tiny, black insects which suck buds, flowers and leaves leaving a silvery streak. They are often found on pelargoniums, fuschias and begonias, and particularly on the flowers which become disfigured. To remove thrips, shake the plant over some newspaper. When the thrips fall out, they can be burnt. Spray the plant with malathion or derris insecticide. It is wise to remove affected flowers and leaves.

White fly White fly are small, white moth-like insects that attack the underside of leaves. They are unsightly, but it is the greenish larvae which do the damage. They suck the sap and deposit a sticky honeydew. Badly infested leaves turn yellow and drop off. The flies spread rapidly from plant to plant, so take care, for they are difficult to get rid of. Spray every three days with a nicotine, malathion or derris insecticide.

A-Z of house plants

■ Easy ● Medium ◆ Difficult

Aechmea fasciata
Bottlebrush plant ■
Description: A rosette of stiff
foliage with a lime like
deposit on the leaves which
should not be removed. A
central flower spike has
small mauve flowers. *Light:*
Tolerant. *Temperature:*
Minimum 13°C (55°F).
Compost: Unimportant as it
only serves as an anchor.
Water: Keep fresh water in
central funnel. Water roots
sparingly. *Feed:* None.
Propagation: By offshoots.
Pests: Untroubled.

Aglaonema modestum
Chinese evergreen ■
Description: Long, narrow
green leaves with lighter
markings and an
insignificant white
arum-like flower. *Light:* Very
tolerant. *Temperature:*
Minimum 13°C (55°F).

Compost: Good-strength
loam-based compost is best.
Water: Twice a week in
summer; once in winter.
Feed: Every 14 days in
summer. *Propagation:* By
division. *Pests:* Scale and
mealy bug. The plant reacts
very badly to gas fumes.

Ananas comosus variegatus
Pineapple ■
Description: A rosette of sharp stiff green and yellow leaves with toothed edges. The flower and fruit spike appear in the centre. *Light:* Colouring improves with light. *Temperature:* Keep warm in winter or rosette will rot. *Compost:* Loam-based J.I. No. 2. *Water:* Once or twice a week in summer and less often in winter, filling rosette with water and moistening soil. *Feed:* If plant starts to fruit. *Propagation:* Produces side shoots. *Pests:* Mealy bug.

Aralia japonica
False castor oil plant ■
Description: Hardy with finger-shaped leaves on a central stem. *Light:* Prefers a light, well ventilated position. *Temperature:* Minimum 10°C (50°F). *Compost:* J.I. No. 2. *Water:* Twice weekly in summer; once in winter. *Feed:* Every 14 days in summer. *Propagation:* From seed or stem cuttings. *Pests:* Greenfly, red spider.

Araucaria excelsa

Norfolk Island Pine ■

Description: Grows to 150 cm (5 ft) tall with a central stem and horizontal branches of soft needles. *Light:* Likes a good light position but can be moved to the shade for short periods. *Temperature:* Minimum 7°C (45°F). *Compost:* J.I. No. 2 or 3 according to size. *Water:* Twice weekly in summer; keep soil just damp in winter. *Feed:* Every 14 days in summer with half recommended dose. *Propagation:* By seed. *Pests:* Mealy bug and greenfly.

Asparagus plumosus

Asparagus fern ■

Description: This plant is not really a fern, but its long feathery fronds often mean that it is taken for one. *Light:* Tolerant of shade. *Temperature:* Minimum 7°C (45°F). *Compost:* Loam- or peat-based. *Water:* Give plenty of water two to three times a week in summer and once in winter. *Feed:* Half the recommended dose every 14 days in summer. *Propagation:* Normally by seed, but big old plants can be divided. *Pests:* Scale and red spider.

Aspidistra eliator
Cast iron plant ■
Description: Very hardy.
Dark green spear-shaped
leaves grow on tall stems.
Occasional purple flowers at
soil level. *Light:* Very
tolerant. You can keep this
plant in almost any position
though it does prefer good
light. *Temperature:*
Minimum 10°C (50°F).
Compost: Soil or
peat-based. *Water:* Twice a
week in summer; once in
winter. *Feed:* Once monthly
in summer.
Propagation: By division.
Pests: Mealy bug, red
spider and scale.

Asplenium nidus avis
Bird's nest fern ■
Description: A rosette of
broad pale green leaves with
brown spines. *Light:* Prefers
draught-free shade.
Temperature: Minimum
13°C (55°F). *Compost:*
Peat-based. *Water:* Once or
twice a week. *Feed:* Half the
recommended dose every
14 days in summer.
Propagation: By spores
which grow under the
fronds. Difficult.
Pests: Scale.

55

Azalea indica
Azalea ■

Description: A compact shrub with small oval leaves that is covered in bright pink, red, mauve and white flowers. Forced to flower from early winter onwards. Place outside after flowering. *Light:* Likes good light and a daily overhead spray. *Temperature:* Minimum 13°C (55°F). *Compost:* Peat-based. *Water:* Plunge in a bucket twice weekly when flowering. *Feed:* In summer ever 14 days. *Propagation:* By stem tip cuttings. *Pests:* Red spider, leaf miner.

Begonia schwabenland
Flowering begonia ■

Description: An all-year round flowering houseplant. *Light:* Enjoys good light but tolerates dark for short periods. *Temperature:* Minimum 15°C (60°F). *Compost:* Loam-based. *Water:* Two to three times a week in flower, every 7-10 days in winter. *Feed:* Once a month in flower. *Propagation:* From seed, leaf or stem cuttings. *Pests:* Mildew, greenfly.

Cacti and Succulents ■
Description:
Exotically-shaped fleshy
plants which store water.
Light: Very tolerant, but
some types grow spectacular
flowers in good light.
Temperature: Minimum 5°C
(40°F). They like any
amount of heat in summer.

Compost: 50%
loam-based, 50% sharp
sand. *Water:* Twice a week in
summer, once a month in
winter. *Feed:* Every
14 days in summer.
Propagation: Usually
by seed.
Pests: Mealy bug. Cactus
spines can be poisonous.

Chamaedorea elegans
Parlour palm ■
Description: A dainty
miniature palm. Small
yellow flowers appear on a
spike straight from the soil.
Light: Keep out of midday
sun. *Temperature:* Keep
cool. Minimum 13°C
(55°F). *Compost:*
Peat-based. *Water:* Two to
three times a week in
summer; once in winter.
Feed: Every 14 days in
summer with half the
recommended dose.
Propagation: By seed.
Pests: Red spider.

Chlorophytum comosum
Spider plant ■

Description: Strap-like leaves, usually green with a cream stripe, grow to 46 cm (18 in) long. Small white flowers produce young plantlets. *Light:* Tolerates shade but prefers good light. *Temperature:* Minimum 10°C (50°F). *Compost:* Rich, loam-based. *Water:* Two to three times a week in summer; once in winter. *Feed:* Every 14 days in summer. *Propagation:* Young plantlets take root in water. *Pests:* Red spider, greenfly.

Chrysanthemum indicum
Chrysanthemum ■

Description: Usually bought in flower or with bud showing colour. Available in many colours. *Light:* Flourish best in good light but avoid midday sun. *Temperature:* Room temperature. *Compost:* Plant in the garden after flowering. *Water:* Every other day. *Feed:* Not necessary. *Propagation:* Cuttings can be taken from fresh shoots. *Pests:* White fly and chrysanthemum virus.

Clivia miniata
Kaffir lily ■

Description: Long glossy strap-shaped leaves bend out from centre. In spring a tall flower spike bears a cluster of orange or yellow trumpet-shaped flowers. *Light:* Tolerant. Place in good light when flower appears. *Temperature:* Minimum 7°C (45°F). *Compost:* Loam-based. *Water:* Once a week when in flower in summer; every 14 days in winter. *Feed:* Weekly when growing. *Propagation:* By division or from young plantlets or seed. *Pests:* Mealy bug and scale.

Cocos weddeliana
Dwarf coconut palm ■

Description: Supple stems bear slender spiky leaves. Grown two or three to a pot. *Light:* Prefers a sunny position. *Temperature:* Minimum 18°C (65°F). *Compost:* Three parts loam to one part peat. *Water:* Twice a week in summer. Keep the root ball just moist in winter. *Feed:* Half the recommended dose every 21 days in summer. *Propagation:* By seed. Difficult. *Pests:* Untroubled.

Cryptanthus bivittatus
Star fish ■
Description: A family of low flat narrow-leaved bromeliads which grow tied firmly to bark or wood. *Light:* Colours are more striking in good light. *Temperature:* Minimum 15°C (60°F). *Compost:* Peat with sphagnum moss added. *Water:* Two to three times a week in summer; once in winter. Water in funnel unnecessary. *Feed:* Not necessary. *Propagation:* Plantlets grow between the leaves of the mature plant.
Pests: No real problems.

Dieffenbachia exotica
Dumb cane ■
Description: Broad variegated leaves grow upwards from a central stem. Mature plants bear small green flowers. *Light:* Tolerates shade. *Temperature:* Minimum 10°C (50°F). *Compost:* J.I. No. 3. *Water:* Twice a week in summer; once in winter. *Feed:* Monthly in summer. *Propagation:* From basal cuttings or top shoots. *Pests:* Mealy bug, red spider.

Dracaena
Dragon tree ■

Description: Strap-like leaves, striped green and cream or red. *Light:* Prefers good light away from the midday sun. *Temperature:* Minimum 15°C (60°F). *Compost:* Either loam- or peat-based. *Water:* Do not over-water or allow to dry out. Once or twice a week in summer; once in winter. *Feed:* Every 14 days in summer. *Propagation:* By tip cuttings or stem or root sections. *Pests:* Red spider, fungus, mealy bug.

Euphorbia pulcherrima
Poinsettia ■

Description: A Christmas-flowering plant with red, pink or white bracts and small yellow flowers. *Light:* Needs good light. *Temperature:* Minimum 13°C (55°F). *Compost:* Often discarded after flowering, but if repotting use peat-based compost. *Water:* Twice a week when in colour. Then give a rest period of four weeks, then water once a week. *Feed:* When growing every 14 days. *Propagation:* By cuttings. *Pests:* Greenfly, silver leaf virus.

61

Fatshedera lizei
Ivy tree ■

Description: A hybrid
between ivy and the castor
oil plant with the leaves of
the former and the upright
growth of the latter.
Light: Tolerates shade.
Temperature: Minimum
10°C (50°F).
Compost: Loam-based.
Water: Two to three times
a week in summer;
once a week in winter.
Feed: In summer every
14 days.
Propagation: By stem
tip cuttings.
Pests: Very susceptible
to red spider.

Ficus benjamina
Weeping fig ■

Description: An elegant
plant with small oval leaves
growing on woody stems
which arch gracefully. *Light:*
Needs a good light position.
Temperature: Minimum
15°C (60°F). *Compost:*
Loam-based No. 2. *Water:*
Once or twice a week in
summer and every 7-10
days in winter. *Feed:* Every
14 days in summer.
Propagation: By stem tip
cuttings. *Pests:* Red spider
and scale.

Ficus elastica robusta
Rubber plant ■
Description: Large leathery oval leaves grow from a woody central stem. Often branches to form a young tree. *Light:* Shade is tolerated but restricts growth. *Temperature:* Minimum 15°C (60°F). *Compost:* Loam-based. *Water:* Once a week in summer; every 10 days in winter. Do not water if leaves turn yellow. *Feed:* Every 14 days in summer. *Propagation:* By air layering. *Pests:* Scale, mealy bug and red spider.

Guzmania minor
Scarlet star ■
Description: Short narrow leaves form a central rosette of orange or red bracts containing tiny white flowers. *Light:* Avoid midday sun. *Temperature:* Minimum 15°C (60°F).

Compost: Peat-based with sphagnum moss added. *Water:* Two or three times a week in summer; once in winter. Keep 2.5 cm (1 in) water in central funnel of plant. *Feed:* Unnecessary. *Propagation:* By offshoots. *Pests:* Greenfly, aphids.

63

Hippeastrum
Amaryllis lily ■
Description: A large bulb
which produces a tall flower
spike with five to six
trumpet-shaped flowers in
red, white or pink in spring.
Light: Tolerant, but flower
colour is best in good light.
Temperature: Minimum
10°C (50°F).
Compost: Loam-based.
Water: Water well while
growing but allow to dry
out when leaves die down.
Feed: Every 14 days
in flower.
Propagation: From
offshoots taken when
repotting.
Pests: Mealy bug.

Hydrangea microphylla
Hydrangea ■
Description: A summer
visitor to the house.
Beautiful mop heads of pink
or blue flowers are borne on
stems with pale green oval
leaves below.
Light: Needs good light.
Temperature: Minimum

7°C (45°F).
Compost: Loam- or
peat-based. *Water:* Plunge
in a bucket three times a
week in summer; every 10
days in winter. *Feed:* Every
seven days when flowering.
Propagation: By stem tip
cuttings. *Pests:* Red spider,
greenfly, fungus.

Impatiens sultanii
Busy Lizzie ■

Description: Fleshy stems with small, green, oval leaves and flat red, pink, orange or white flowers. Variegated types are also found. *Light:* Flourishes best in full sun.

Temperature: Minimum 13°C (55°F).

Compost: Rich, loam-based No. 3. *Water:* Two to three times a week in summer; every 10 days in winter.

Feed: Once a week in summer.

Propagation: From seed or by stem tip cuttings.

Pests: Greenfly, red spider, sooty mould.

Kalanchoe blossfeldiana
Ice plant ■

Description: Masses of compact fleshy leaves with clusters of bright flowers on short stems above them. Flowers are usually red, but also pink, yellow and mauve. *Light:* Full during winter, avoid sun in summer.

Temperature: Minimum 13°C (55°F). *Compost:* Loam-based. *Water:* Once a week in summer; every 10-14 days in winter.

Feed: Once a month when growing.

Propagation: By seed or young cuttings.

Pests: Mildew.

Kentia forsteriana
Paradise palm ■
Description: A popular palm
with tall fronds and
gracefully arching leaves.
Often potted in groups.
Light: Tolerates heavy
shade. *Temperature:*
Minimum 15°C (60°F).
Compost: Loam-based No.
2 with 25% extra peat
added. *Water:* Twice a week
in summer; every 10-14
days in winter. Never allow it
to dry out. *Feed:* Every 14
days in summer.
Propagation: From imported
seeds. Difficult. *Pests:* Red
spider, scale.

Monstera deliciosa
Mexican bread plant ■
Description: Has large,
deeply cut and holed leaves.
When fairly mature it
produces a seed pod with
edible pulp around the seed.
Light: Tolerates shade.
Avoid direct sun.
Temperature: Minimum
15°C (60°F). *Compost:*
Peat-based. *Water:* Once a
week in summer; every 14
days in winter. *Feed:* Every
14 days in summer.
Propagation: By stem leaf
cuttings. *Pests:* Red spider.

Neoregelia carolinae
Cartwheel plant ■
Description: A large flat rosette of saw-edged green and cream leaves produces red bracts and small mauve flowers. *Light:* Tolerates periods of shade. *Temperature:* Minimum 15°C (60°F). *Compost:* 50% peat, 50% loam. *Water:* Keep centre filled with water at all times. *Feed:* Half the recommended dose every 14 days in the funnel in summer.
Propagation: By offshoots. *Pests:* Scale.

Pelargonium
Geranium ■
Description: The zonal geranium has irregular, round leaves which are often prettily marked. *Light:* Needs the full light of a window. *Temperature:* Maximum 10°C (50°F). *Compost:* Peat- or loam-based. *Water:* Two to three times a week in summer; every 14 days in winter.
Feed: Every 14 days when growing.
Propagation: By stem cuttings.
Pests: Whitefly, fungus and leafy gall.

Philodendron scandens
Sweetheart plant ■
Description: A climbing plant with heart-shaped leaves that needs support but also looks good in a hanging basket.
Light: Gets straggly without good light.
Temperature: Minimum 15°C (60°F).
Compost: Either peat- or loam-based.
Water: Twice a week in summer and once in winter.
Feed: Every 14 days in summer. *Propagation:* Either from seed or stem cuttings. A suitable plant for hydroculture. *Pests:* Greenfly, mealy bug and red spider.

Phoenix canariensis
Canary date palm ■
Description: A large palm with spreading spiky leaves.
Light: Tolerates the dark but grows better in good light and air. Can be put outside in summer. *Temperature:* Minimum 10°C (50°F).
Compost: Rich, peat-based.
Water: Two to three times a week in summer; every 14 days in winter. *Feed:* Every 14 days in summer.
Propagation: From seeds or date stones. *Pests:* Mealy bug.

Platycerium alcicorne
Stag's head fern ■
Description: Long, thick
finger-like fronds emerge
from sterile back leaves. The
fronds are covered with
down which should not be
removed. *Light:* Tolerant of
the dark. *Temperature:*
Minimum 15°C (60°F).
Compost: Peat-based mixed
with sphagnum moss.
Water: Plunge in water every
week in summer and every
10 days in winter. *Feed:*
Every 14 days in summer.
Propagation: By spores or
offshoots. *Pests:* Scale.

Primula vulgaris
Primrose ■
Description: A hybrid of the
familiar hedgerow primrose
with soft-coloured flowers.
Primulas with mauve and
pink flowers are also
available. *Light:* Needs a
well-lit position.
Temperature: Keep cool.
Compost: Plant in the
garden after flowering to
naturalize.
Water: Two to three times a
week. *Feed:* Once a week
when in flower. *Propagation:*
By seed or division.
Pests: Greenfly.

Rhoicissus rhomboidea
Grape ivy ■

Description: A good fast-growing climbing plant with small beech-type leaves and brown tentacles. *Light:* Prefers good northern light. *Temperature:* Minimum 15°C (60°F). *Compost:* Loam-based No. 2. *Water:* About twice a week in summer and every 14 days in winter. *Feed:* Every 14 days in summer. *Propagation:* By young leaf and tip shoots. *Pests:* Greenfly and red spider.

Sansevieria trifasciata
Mother-in-law's tongue ■

Description: Long thick sword-like leaves, fleshy in texture and green and yellow in colour, emerge straight from the soil. Sometimes has a small yellow flower spike. *Light:* Very tolerant. *Temperature:* Minimum 10°C (50°F). *Compost:* Loam-based. *Water:* Do not over-water. Every 7-10 days in summer; every 14 days in winter. *Feed:* Every 21 days in summer. *Propagation:* By division or leaf sections. *Pests:* Mealy bug.

Schefflera actinophylla
Umbrella tree ■
Description: Long oval leaves arranged in groups of four or five at the end of tall stems. *Light:* Likes good light away from direct sun. *Temperature:* Minimum 13°C (55°F). *Compost:* Loam-based J.I. No. 1. *Water:* Two or three times a week in summer; once in winter. *Feed:* Half the recommended dose every 14 days in summer. *Propagation:* From seed or cuttings. A good subject for hydroculture. *Pests:* Red spider, scale and mealy bug.

Tradescantia fluminensis
Wandering Jew ■
Description: Long trailing stems with small green oval leaves which can be variegated. *Light:* Becomes leggy without good light. *Temperature:* Minimum 10°C (50°F). *Compost:* Loam- or peat-based. *Water:* Twice a week in summer; once in winter. *Feed:* Every 14 days in summer. *Propagation:* By stem cuttings. *Pests:* Greenfly.

71

Vriesia splendens
Flaming sword ■
Description: A rosette of green and brown striped leaves. A central flower spike turns bright orange and displays small yellow flowers. *Light:* Tolerant. *Temperature:* Minimum 18°C (65°F). *Compost:* Peat-based. *Water:* Keep compost damp and centre of rosette full.
Feed: Half the recommended dose every 14 days in summer.
Propagation: By offshoots which appear after the parent plant has flowered.
Pests: Red spider

Yucca elephantipes
Spineless yucca ■
Description: Rosettes of stiff sword-like leaves on the top or sides of mature woody canes.
Light: Fairly tolerant.
Temperature: Minimum 8°C (47°F). *Compost:*
Soil-based. Anchor well.
Water: Two to three times a week in summer; every 10 days in winter. *Feed:* Half the recommended dose every week in summer.
Propagation: By sections of cane. *Pests:* Scale, mealy bug and botrytis.

Adiantum capillus veneris
Maiden hair fern ●
Description: Delicate pale green foliage droops gracefully. *Light:* Keep out of direct sunlight.
Temperature: Minimum 10°C (50°F). *Compost:* Peat-based. *Water:* Keep well watered. Spray daily.

Feed: Half the recommended dose every 14 days in summer.
Propagation: By division or from spores.
Pests: Resistant to most pests. If plant dries out, cut off dead fronds and water well — new shoots will quickly appear.

Aphelandra squarrosa
Zebra plant ●
Description: Oval-shaped green leaves with cream or silver vein markings and bright yellow bracts. *Light:* Avoid midday sun.
Temperature: Minimum 15°C (60°F). *Compost:* J.I.

No. 3. *Water:* Two to three times a week in summer and once in winter. *Feed:* Every 14 days when flower spike appears.
Propagation: From cuttings.
Pests: Red spider, greenfly and scale.

73

Beloperone guttata
Shrimp plant ●
Description:
Peach-coloured bracts and small white flowers give this plant its common name. Oval leaves grow in pairs. *Light:* Full sunlight in summer; indirect light in winter. *Temperature:* 7°C (45°F). *Compost:* Loam-based. *Water:* Once or twice a week in summer; every 14 days in winter. *Feed:* Every 14 days in summer. *Propagation:* By tip cuttings. *Pests:* Red spider and greenfly.

Bougainvillea glabra
Paper flower ●
Description: Small, green, oval leaves and bright mauve bracts on very woody stems. *Light:* Needs bright sun. *Temperature:* Minimum 5°C (40°F). *Compost:* Rich, loam-based. *Water:* Up to three times a week in summer; every 7-10 days in winter. *Feed:* Half the recommended dose every 14 days in summer. *Propagation:* By cuttings, but difficult. *Pests:* Red spider, scale, mealy bug.

Campanula isophylla
Bell flower ●
Description: In summer covered with a mass of white or pale mauve flowers. *Light:* Needs good light. Avoid midday sun. *Temperature:* Minimum 6°C (43°F). *Compost:* Loam-based.

Water: Check daily in summer; water every 7-10 days in winter. *Feed:* Every 14 days in summer. Cut back in winter. *Propagation:* Use prunings as cuttings. *Pests:* Red spider, greenfly.

Cissus antarctica
Kangaroo vine ●
Description: A good green climbing plant with oval, serrated edge leaves. Related to the rhoicissus but less tolerant. *Light:* Needs good light. Avoid midday sun. *Temperature:* Minimum 13°C (55°F). *Compost:* Loam-based. *Water:* Not more than twice a week in summer and every 14 days in winter. *Feed:* Every 14 days in summer. *Propagation:* By stem tips. *Pests:* Red spider and greenfly.

Citrus mitis

Miniature orange ●

Description: Small oval privet-like leaves grow on a multi-branched stem. Sweetly scented flowers produce a small bright orange fruit which is edible but bitter. *Light:* Needs good light and air.

Temperature: Minimum 5°C (40°F).

Compost: Loam-based.

Water: Three to four times a week in sumrner; every 10 days in winter.

Feed: Every 14 days in summer.

Propagation: Difficult.

Pests: Mealy bug, scale, white fly, mould.

Cleorodendron thomsonae

Bleeding heart vine ●

Description: A climber with dark green glossy heart-shaped leaves. The spectacular flowers are dark red. *Light:* Needs good light and humidity. Prefers greenhouse conditions.

Temperature: Minimum 13°C (55°F). *Compost:* Loam-based. *Water:* Twice a week in summer; every 10 days in winter.

Feed: Every 21 days in summer.

Propagation: By seed or stem tip cuttings. *Pests:* Red spider, greenfly.

Coffea arabica
Coffee plant ●
Description: A dense shrub with glossy, dark green leaves growing to 120 cm (4 ft), but unlikely to bear coffee beans.
Light: Avoid midday sun in summer; in winter place in full light.
Temperature:
Minimum 15°C (60°F).
Compost: Loam-based.
Water: Twice a week in summer; every 10 days in winter.
Feed: Every 14 days in summer.
Propagation: By seed or side shoots.
Pests: Greenfly, red spider.

Cordyline terminalis
Cabbage palm ●
Description: Upright with red, green or cream, long spear-shaped leaves, growing from a central stem.
Light: Good light preferred, but avoid midday sun.
Temperature: Minimum 18°C (65°F). *Compost:* Loam-based with extra peat.
Water: Once or twice a week in summer; every 7-10 days in winter. *Feed:* Every 14 days in summer.
Propagation: By stem cuttings or stem or root sections. *Pests:* Red spider, greenfly, scale.

Crossandra undulaefolia
Crossandra ●
Description: A compact plant with dark green leaves and orange flowers. *Light:* A good light position away from the midday sun. *Temperature:* Minimum 15°C (60°F). *Compost:* Loam-based. *Water:* Use tepid water. Keep plant on dry side: once a week in summer and every 14 days in winter. *Feed:* Every 14 days in summer. *Propagation:* By stem tip cuttings or seed. *Pests:* Greenfly, red spider.

Cyclamen persicum
Cyclamen ●
Description: Round leaves and delicately coloured flowers come from a central corm. *Light:* Good light. Avoid midday sun. *Temperature:* Keep at 7-15°C (45-60°F), falling at night to −12°C (10°F). *Compost:* Loam-based. *Water:* From below, twice a week when growing, otherwise once. Allow to dry out for six weeks in early summer. *Feed:* Every 14 days when growing. *Propagation:* By seed. *Pests:* Greenfly, botrytis.

Cyperus diffusus

Umbrella grass ●

Description: Grassy leaves and brown whispy flowers in an umbrella-shape at the top of tall stems. *Light:* Likes good light but avoid midday sun. *Temperature:* Minimum 15°C (60°F). *Compost:* Loam-based. *Water:* Pot should be standing in a little water at all times. Water three times a week all year round. *Feed:* Every 14 days when growing. *Propagation:* By division. *Pests:* Green- and white fly.

Fuschia ●

Description: Each of the many varieties has lovely pendant flowers, often with bell and petals of contrasting colours. All have protruding stamens. *Light:* Needs direct light from a window. *Temperature:* Minimum 7°C (45°F). *Compost:* Loam-based. *Water:* Three to four times a week in summer; can be allowed to dry out in winter. *Feed:* Weekly when in flower. *Propagation:* From cuttings or seed. *Pests:* Greenfly.

79

Grevillea robusta
Silk oak ●

Description: An evergreen shrub which grows like a young tree with feathery foliage from a central stem. *Light:* Needs a good light position but avoid midday sun. *Temperature:* Minimum 7°C (45°F). *Compost:* Loam-based. *Water:* Twice a week in summer; once in winter. *Feed:* Every 14 days in summer. *Propagation:* By seed or stem cuttings. *Pests:* Red spider and mealy bug.

Hedera helix
Ivy ●

Description: Variegated and mutated ivies are very popular and vary greatly in size.
Light: They need plenty of light and a humid atmosphere. Not tolerant of central heating.
Temperature: Minimum 7°C (45°F). *Compost:* Peat- or loam-based. *Water:* Once or twice a week in summer and once in winter. Spray daily in hot weather.
Feed: Every 14 days in summer.
Propagation: By leaf cuttings in spring.
Pests: Greenfly, scale, red spider and mould.

80

Hibiscus rosa-sinensis
Rose of China ●
Description: Dark green
serrated leaves and a
succession of short-lived
flowers, varying in colour
from deep red to pure yellow.
Light: Needs good light.
Temperature: Minimum
10°C (50°F). *Compost:*
Loam-based with added
peat. *Water:* Twice a week in
summer; once in winter.
Feed: Every 14 days in
summer.
Propagation: By cuttings
or air layering.
Pests: Greenfly.

Hoya carnosa
Wax flower ●
Description: A climbing
plant with oblong leaves.
Bunches of pink star-shaped
flowers drop a honey-like
liquor. *Light:* Needs good
light but avoid midday sun.
Temperature: Minimum
10°C (50°F). *Compost:*
Soil-based compost on
crushed brick. *Water:* Once
a week in summer; every 14
days in winter. *Feed:* Half
the recommended dose
every three to four weeks
in summer.
Propagation: By stem
tip cuttings.
Pests: Mealy bug,
red spider.

81

Maranta mackoyana

Prayer plant ●

Description: Colourful leaves normally have a green background with vein and spine markings in cream, red, black or brown. The leaves curl at night, looking like praying hands.

Light: Avoid direct sun.

Temperature: Minimum 10°C (50°F).

Compost: Peat-based.

Water: Two to three times a week in summer; once in winter.

Feed: Half the recommended dose every 14 days in summer.

Propagation: By division of roots.

Pests: Red spider.

A

B

Orchids ●

Description: Cymbidium (A) blooms in late winter with spikes of up to 20 flowers; Paphiopedilum (B), the slipper orchid, flowers in late summer with single flowers from a bed of small leaves.

Light: Avoid midday sun.

Temperature: Minimum 10°C (50°F).

Compost: Orchid compost.

Water: Two to three times a week when flowering, then allow to rest.

Feed: Once a week in flower.

Propagation: By division.

Pests: Thrips, scale.

Peperomia magnoliaefolia
Desert privet ●
Description: Privet-like leaves are green with a cream edging. Compact bushy plants. *Light:* Avoid dark places and bright sun. *Temperature:* Minimum 13°C (55°F).
Compost: Soil-based.
Water: Every 10 days in summer and every 14-18 days in winter.
Feed: Half the recommended dose every 20 days in summer.
Propagation: By stem or leaf cuttings.
Pests: Red spider.

Pilea cadieri
Aluminium plant ●
Description: Delicate plants with fleshy stems bearing dark green leaves with aluminium markings. *Light:* Like good light but avoid midday sun. *Temperature:* Minimum 10°C (50°F).

Compost: Loam-based with 25% extra peat added. *Water:* Two to three times a week in summer; once in winter. *Feed:* The normal dose every 14 days in summer. *Propagation:* By stem tip cuttings. *Pests:* Greenfly and mould rot.

Pteris tremula
Trembling fern ●
Description: Large
branched fronds, with four
to five fingers on each side of
the stem, grow from the
centre of the plant like
bracken. They break easily.
Light: Prefers shade.
Temperature: Minimum
10°C (50°F). *Compost:*
Peat. *Water:* Up to once a
day in summer and twice a
week in winter. *Feed:* Half
the recommended dose
every 14 days in summer.
Propagation: By root division
or spores.
Pests: Scale or insects
on stems.

Saintpaulia ionantha
African violet ●
Description: Soft, almost
round leaves form a circle
round the crown. Pink,
purple or white flowers grow
above them. *Light:* Needs
good light away
from midday sun.
Temperature:

Minimum 13°C (55°F).
Compost: Peat-based.
Water: Keep moist all year
round. Water from bottom of
pot twice weekly.
Feed: Every three to
four weeks when growing.
Propagation: By seed or
leaf cuttings.
Pests: Greenfly, mould.

Scindapsus aureus
Devil's ivy ●
Description: A climbing or trailing plant with aerial roots and heart-shaped green and cream leaves.
Light: Good light out of the midday sun.
Temperature: Minimum 13°C (55°F).
Compost: Loam-based.
Water: Every four to five days in summer; weekly in winter.
Feed: Half the recommended dose every 14 days in summer.
Propagation: By stem cuttings.
Pests: Red spider.

Sinningia speciosa
Gloxinia ●
Description: Large leaves and red, pink or mauve trumpet-shaped flowers.
Light: Needs good light. Avoid midday sun.
Temperature: Keep tubers frost free in winter and at 21°C (70°F) in spring to promote growth. *Compost:* Peat-based. *Water:* From below two to three times a week in summer. Allow to dry out in winter.
Feed: Once a week in summer.
Propagation: By seed.
Pests: Greenfly, spotted wilt.

85

Spathiphyllum wallisii
Sail plant ●
Description: Bright green lance-shaped leaves on stems which sprout from the centre of the plant. Throws out a long-lasting white flower with a yellow central spadix.
Light: Needs semi-shade in summer and full light in winter.
Temperature: Minimum 15°C (60°F). *Compost:* J.I. No. 3 with 25% peat added.
Water: Two to three times a week in summer; once in winter. *Feed:* Every 14 days in summer. *Propagation:* By seed or division. *Pests:* Greenfly, red spider.

Streptocarpus hybridus
Cape primrose ●
Description: Long strap-like leaves and four to five mauve, pink, white or mixed flowers. *Light:* Needs good light out of midday sun.
Temperature: Minimum 15°C (60°F). *Compost:* Peat-based. *Water:* Two to three times a week in summer; once in winter.
Feed: Half the recommended dose once a month. *Propagation:* By seed or leaf cuttings. *Pests:* Greenfly.

Syngonium podophyllum
Goose foot plant ●
Description: A climbing
plant with green
triangular leaves.
Leaf changes shape
as the plant matures.
Needs to be tied to a stake.
Light: Avoid midday sun.
Temperature: Minimum
15°C (60°F).
Compost: Loam-based with
25% peat added.
Water: Two to three times
a week in summer; once
in winter.
Feed: Half the
recommended dose every
21 days in summer.
Propagation: By stem
cuttings. *Pests:* Greenfly,
red spider.

Tetrastigma voinierianum
Chestnut vine ●
Description: A large, fragile,
quick-growing vine with
slightly serrated, pointed
oval leaves. Needs support.
Light: Needs good light but
avoid midday sun.
Temperature: Minimum
13°C (55°F). *Compost:*
Loam-based. *Water:* Two to
three times a week in
summer; once in winter.
Feed: Every 14 days in
summer. *Propagation:* By
stem tip cuttings.
Pests: Red spider, greenfly.

87

Anthurium scherzerianum
Flamingo flower ◆
Description: Long, narrow leaves grow from the centre. The flower is on a long stem and has a flat red, white, pink or yellow bract with a curly flower cluster. *Light:* Needs good light.
Temperature: Minimum 18°C (65°F). *Compost:* Peat-based with $\frac{1}{3}$ chopped sphagnum moss added.
Water: Twice a week in summer; once in winter.
Feed: Every 14 days in summer.
Propagation: Difficult.
Pests: Mealy bug, red spider, fungus.

Begonia rex
Foliage begonia ◆
Description: Its large, irregular-shaped, serrated leaves are multicoloured and delicately patterned. Leaves are fragile. *Light:* Avoid direct sun.
Temperature: Minimum 13°F (55°F). *Compost:* Peat-based. *Water:* Twice a week in summer; every 10 days in winter. *Feed:* Every 14 days in summer.
Propagation: By leaf cuttings.
Pests: Red spider, fungus, mould.

Caladium bicolor
Angel's wings ◆
Description: Broad, paper thin, arrow-shaped leaves are white, red or pink, tinged with green.
Light: Full light away from midday sun.
Temperature: Minimum 13°C (55°F). *Compost:* Rich loam with 25% peat added.
Water: Two to three times a week in summer. Allow to dry out in winter.
Feed: Half the recommended dose every 21 days in summer.
Propagation: By seed or splitting tubers.
Pests: Greenfly.

Codiaeum variegatum
Jacob's coat ◆
Description: Broad brightly coloured leaves or orange, red, yellow and green on single stems. *Light:* The colours are seen to best advantage in full sun.
Temperature: Minimum 15°C (60°F). *Compost:* Loam-based. *Water:* Two to three times a week in summer; once in winter.
Feed: Every 14 days in summer. *Propagation:* By stem tip cuttings. *Pests:* Red spider, mealy bug, scale.

89

Columnea microphylla
Golden vine ◆
Description: Long, trailing
stems are covered with
small, oval leaves and bear
profusions of bright orange
flowers in spring. *Light:*
Needs good light.
Temperature: Minimum
15°C (60°F).
Compost: J.I. No. 1 with
25% peat added.
Water: Twice a week in
summer; once in winter,
except in February. *Feed:*
Every 14 days in summer.
Propagation: By stem tip
cuttings in spring. *Pests:*
Red spider.

Fittonia verschaffeltii
Painted net leaf ◆
Description: Oval leaves
with red and cream
markings with tiny white
flowers. *Light:* Needs
shade. Best grown in a
greenhouse and brought
indoors occasionally.
Temperature: Minimum
18°C (65°F). *Compost:*
Peat- or soil-based. *Water:*
Two or three times a week in
summer, once in winter.
Needs humid conditions.
Feed: Every 14 days with
half the recommended dose
in summer. *Propagation:* By
division or by stem cuttings.
Pests: Greenfly.

Gardenia jasminoides
Gardenia ◆
Description: Small bushy plants with dark green pointed oval leaves and heavily scented creamy white double flowers. *Light:* Needs good light away from midday sun. *Temperature:* Minimum 15°C (60°F).

Compost: Rich loam. *Water:* Three times a week in summer; once in winter. *Feed:* Half the recommended dose every 14 days in summer. *Propagation:* By young stem tip cuttings in spring. *Pests:* Mealy bug, scale, red spider.

Stephanotis floribunda
Madagascar jasmine ◆
Description: A quick growing climbing plant with thick leathery leaves and waxen white flowers carried in clusters. *Light:* Needs maximum light. *Temperature:* Minimum 15°C (60°F). *Compost:* Loam-based. *Water:* Two to three times a week in summer; once in winter. *Feed:* Half the recommended dose every 14 days in summer. *Propagation:* From lateral stem tip cuttings from last year's growth. *Pests:* Scale, red spider and mealy bug.

Glossary

Air layering A method of propagating a single stem-med plant which has lost its lower leaves.

Areole A hairy, cushion-like area found at the base of the spines on cacti.

Bleeding When sap is lost from a plant after it has been cut.

Bract A modified, often brightly coloured leaf which grows near the calyx of a flower.

Bulb An underground bud from which flowers and leaves grow.

Cactus Succulent plant with a thick, fleshy stem. Usually has spines and brightly coloured flowers, but no leaves.

Calyx A ring of leaves around a bud or flower.

Capillary action Natural tendency for water to be drawn upwards.

Coloured leaf Leaf with colours other than green, white or cream. See variegated.

Compost A mixture of peat or loam with other ingredients which supports plant roots in a pot.

Crown Upper part of root often projecting from the surface of soil.

Cutting A leaf or a stem which is used to propagate a plant.

Dormant Period when plant naturally stops growing, usually in winter. Leaves may fall and top growth dies down.

Exotic An unusual and/or striking plant or flower.

F₁ Hybrid Product of two pure bred plants, but itself produces no seed.

Fertilizer Chemical substances used to stimulate and sustain plant growth.

Flower spike Stem on which flowers grow.

Foliar Relating to leaves as in foliar feed which is absorbed through the leaves of a plant.

Forcing Making plants flower earlier than would occur naturally.

Frond The leaf of a palm or fern.

Fungicide Chemical used to kill diseases caused by fungi.

Germination When bulbs or seeds start to grow.

Growing point The tip of a stem from which upward growth occurs.

Growing season Period when plants start to grow again, usually from March to October.

Honeydew A sweet, clear nectar produced by some plants.

Humidity Moisture in atmosphere.

Hybrid Plant produced by two parents of different varieties.

Hygrometer Instrument which measures the amount of water in the air.

Inorganic Term often applied to fertilizer or other chemicals to mean a substance derived from a source which has never been alive. e.g. minerals.

Lateral stems Branches growing out sideways from main stem.

Leaf node The point where leaf joins stem.

Loam Soil which contains clay, sand and rotted vegetable matter.

Micro-climate Climate produced by plants growing close together.

Misting Very fine water spray.

Mutated Branched.

Offshoots Small plants produced by mother plant.

Organic Term often applied to fertilizer or other chemicals to mean a substance derived from a source which has been alive. e.g. rotted vegetable matter

Osmosis The tendency of water to pass through a fine membrane.

Peat Partly decomposed vegetable matter used in composts as it retains moisture.

Pesticide A chemical used to kill pests.

Pinch out To remove the growing point of a stem to encourage the plant to become bushy or to flower.

Plantlet A small plant.

Plunging Watering a plant by placing it up to its rim in water.

Pot-bound When a pot is too small to allow a plant's roots to grow.

Resting period Time when plant growth stops, but leaves do not fall. See dormant.

Rosette Collection of leaves shaped like a rose.

Rootball Collection of fine roots around main central root.

Sap Vital liquid circulating in plants.

Secondary leaves Leaves which appear on a seedling after the first set of leaves.

Sharp sand An ingredient of compost; feels coarse to the touch.

Shrub Woody plant (smaller than a tree) with branches that divide near the ground and no central stem.

Spadix Spike carrying both male and female flowers.

Specimen plant A single large plant which provides a focal point for a room.

Sphagnum moss A water-retaining moss which grows easily. Used for hanging baskets and for orchids.

Spore A tiny cell-like seed from which plants like ferns grow.

Succulent A plant with thick, fleshy leaves and stem which store water.

Systemic A fertilizer or pesticide absorbed into a plant through the leaves or roots.

Top dressing Covering the top of a potted plant's soil with fresh compost.

Variegated Leaf which is green with white, cream or yellow blotches, or edges on it.

Ventilate Expose to the air.

Plant index

Page numbers in italics refer to illustrations; those in bold to entries in the A-Z section.

Index

PDO 81-776